RESCUED!

From New Age Spirituality and Superstition

Copyright © 2023 by **Karis Grace**

All rights reserved. No portion of this publication may be reproduced, stored in an electronic system, or transmitted in any form by any means, electronic, mechanical, photocopy, recording, or otherwise, without the author's prior permission, except in the case of brief quotations used in literary reviews and certain other non-commercial uses permitted by copyright law. For permission requests, write to the contact address below.

The views expressed in this book are the author's and do not necessarily reflect those of the publisher.

Unless otherwise noted, all Scripture quotations in this book are taken from *The New International Version* of The Holy Bible. New International Version®, NIV® Copyright ©1973, 1978, 1984, 2011 by Biblica, Inc.® Used by permission. All rights reserved worldwide.

Scriptures noted as "ISV" are taken from The International Standard Version. Copyright © 1995-2014 by ISV Foundation. ALL RIGHTS RESERVED INTERNATIONALLY. Used by permission of Davidson Press, LLC.

Scriptures noted as "TLB" are taken from The Living Bible. The Living Bible copyright © 1971 by Tyndale House Foundation. Used by permission of Tyndale House Publishers Inc., Carol Stream, Illinois 60188. All rights reserved.

www.WorldwidePublishingGroup.com
7710-T Cherry Park Dr., Ste 224   Houston, Texas 77095
(713) 766-4271

Cover and Book Layout @ 2023 Harvest Creek Publishing and Design

Ordering Information: Special discounts are available on quantity purchases by churches, associations, and others. For details, please contact the author at the address listed.

Rescued!/Karis Grace—1st ed.
ISBN: 978-0-9997837-7-1

Printed in The United States of America

CONTENTS

INTRODUCTION 9

CHAPTER 1: BEGINNING TO SEE THE LIGHT 11

CHAPTER 2: NOTHING NEW ABOUT THE NEW AGE MOVEMENT 23

CHAPTER 3: THE MODERN ROOTS OF THE MOVEMENT 27

CHAPTER 4: WHO IS GOD TO NEW AGERS? 29

CHAPTER 5: WHAT ATTRACTS PEOPLE TO NEW AGE? 33

CHAPTER 6: A DESIRE TO KNOW THE FUTURE 35

CHAPTER 7: A DESIRE TO KNOW THE PAST 49

CHAPTER 8: THE MYSTERY OF NEW AGE 61

CHAPTER 9: NEW AGE HEALING PRACTICES 69

CHAPTER 10: NEW AGE HEALTH APPLICATIONS 83

CHAPTER 11: NEW AGE VS DIVINE REVELATION 97

CHAPTER 12: 10 REASONS WHY THE NEW AGE MOVEMENT IS NOT CHRISTIAN 99

CHAPTER 13: NOT ALL ROADS LEAD TO HEAVEN—THIS ONE DOES! 107

EPILOGUE 109

Never forget that there are only two sources of spiritual power in the universe.

They are God and Satan.

This is a riveting and true story of the rescue of a woman and a family in torment. Where evil had inserted its plan, there was a greater plan of love that stepped in and defeated it all.

INTRODUCTION

Having tried it all. I grew tired of the unfulfilled New Age promises. Everything I tried, once the newness and excitement wore off, left me feeling empty inside. I know I am not alone. I have met others who have experienced the same. It also opened me up to the most tormented time in my life. But thankfully, through the torment, I discovered THE WAY to real life. It wasn't a ritual. It was a person.

I realize this may be a difficult book to read. It may challenge your beliefs, ideas, and even your way of life. I urge you to read it, anyway. Then seek the truth yourself.

I am writing this book for three groups of people.

First, I'm writing to those who, like I was, are deeply involved in New Age concepts and practices. I hope that as you read my experience, you may find hope and the true answer for life and living.

Second, I'm writing to those who are already weary of the journey; You may be tormented yourself and looking for answers. You may know someone who is oppressed. Those who have learned that the New Age life didn't work centuries ago when it was developed, nor does it work today, because it has no true foundation.

Finally, I am writing to those who may dabble in New Age, seeking truth, looking for answers. Who knows that there must be more to life than what they've found thus far, something that will fill the void they feel inside? You are my people. There is hope. May you find it in the truth written on these pages. Here is the good news: You will find the solution you seek here.

- Karis Grace

Chapter 1

Beginning To See the Light

As I lay on the couch, I felt an unseen presence. Like a cat pulling at fabric with its paws, it felt like a cat had pounced on the couch and was picking its paws up through the fabric of the couch, one paw at a time. This was not the first time I had felt something that was not obvious to everyone else around me, but this was the time that it made me so uncomfortable that I started to question what was going on.

Then I felt an unseen presence plop down on the couch next to me. It was as if a person had just sat down. I could sense their weightiness, but no one was physically there. I heard a familiar voice speak to me. It was my ex-husband's voice, though, in reality, he was many miles away. I heard him plainly, as it seemed he had cuddled up next to me. I am sure I was missing him and still pining for him, hoping things would be different and he and I would get back together.

I was visualizing in my mind what I wanted from a future husband, so it would manifest. But this invisible appearance took me aback. Somehow, even though I was trying to create what I wanted, this frightened me. That was because I truly knew it was not really him. He had moved on with his life. Even though this manifestation seemed like him, somehow, I knew it wasn't.

I had not been frightened by the typing on the computer from the other room when I was in the house alone; or when the television mysteriously turned itself off and on. Nor was I frightened when the odd noises in my house became commonplace. Somehow, I was able to explain away what I was seeing and hearing.

After all the reading I had done, I believed in angels and assumed these entities must be angelic, as I did not believe in hell. Furthermore, why would anything hellish have anything to do with me? I was a good person, and these things, making themselves increasingly known, were all good to me. I had no idea how dark and sinister they truly were.

Why was I so concerned *now* when my children previously telling me they were afraid, had not done so? When my son told me his blanket flew off his bed or that something was grabbing his legs and pulling him off the bed, it was easy to discount. He was a six-year-old who did not want to go to bed.

Frankly, it sounded like some *Harry Potter* adventure or game he was in was coming to life in our home. I was tired and just wanted him to go to bed so I could have "my time."
It was not when the lights flickered off and on or when one light bulb broke into a thousand pieces as I walked by. But those things were becoming harder to deny. Something abnormal was going on in my life, and it was time for me to confront it. No, not yet. There would have to be a few more incidents to convince me what I was seeing and experiencing was a problem.

One night, my then three-year-old and I were in her bedroom. She was playing and wanted me to play with her. Suddenly she looked up, pointed to the playroom outside of her bedroom, and said, "Mommy, look at the big smoke," pointing into her playroom where she had just been. I looked and saw what she was talking about. It appeared to be the smoky image of a person. We continued to play because we had seen it before and knew it would go away if we ignored it.

It seemed things like this were showing up more and more. Foolishly, I thought, *how great. I could see angels, and my kids could see them too.* This was exciting, yet I knew to keep this to myself. After all, who would believe me? And if they did, they might consider this merely a schizophrenic episode requiring medication. I would not share with many people the things that were going on in my and my children's lives for fear of being called crazy. And it was crazy. How could all three of us be having the same psychotic break, with the same psychotic episodes at the same time?

Yet I could not imagine the war that would break out. Nor could I have expected all hell, using whatever means necessary, would soon torment my mind and body to shut me up. What was going on in my home? What kind of portal had I opened that allowed these things to saturate our home?

Was I mentally ill? Schizophrenic? Even if so, how could my children experience the same psychotic episodes at the same time I was? And who could help me? I couldn't tell anyone; they would surely think I was a mental case. I had no one to turn to. One sleepless night led to another.

One night while lying in bed, I felt the weightiness of something on top of me. I was very aware of its presence. I turned over and pulled the blankets over my eyes and tried to hide from it. It blew its breath in my face, and I opened my eyes to see a grotesque creature looking at me. Instantly, I instinctively said, "Get behind me, Satan!" Immediately, the creature jumped off me.

At that moment, I cried out to Jesus. I had not spoken His name in years. I was not going to church, reading the bible, or engaged in any relationship with Him. But the moment I called His name, He showed up. Instantly... in my bedroom! I knew then that I was safe.

But to my surprise, the grotesque creature did not leave. Even with Jesus in the room, it stood there. That is when Jesus said to me, "Tell it to leave. You invited it in." I was shocked to hear this. How had I invited this monster into my home and onto my bed? But somehow, I knew I had. And it had not left; it was still there.

I said, "Jesus, I need angels." Instantly I saw two angels standing face-to-face with the dark creature between them. I said, "Jesus, I need more angels." At that point, the entire room was filled with angels, with no space left. Still, the demon remained.

I looked at Jesus, a bit confused. He said again, "You invited it in. You tell it to leave." So, I did. I told it to leave, and the two angels escorted it right out.

But it would come back. I felt this intense evil presence coming from a distance, and I immediately knew it was coming for me. Just as it reached for my throat, an angel stepped in and wrestled it off me. It left.

This happened a few more times than I care to remember. An angel would always show up at what seemed like the last possible moment and step in front of what was attacking me. Other times, I would awaken in the night, paralyzed but awake. Again, an evil presence covered my mouth and nose, and I could not move or scream. I would try to move my mouth, but it would not move. I tried my hardest to say "Jesus" and would keep at it until, finally, something would break, and the paralysis would subside.

Another night, I felt the presence of a dead loved one at the foot of my bed, along with a dog that had also passed away. They were trying to provoke me to interact with them. I grabbed my Bible and began to read it. But I hadn't read it long before an overwhelming sleepiness consumed me. I felt as if I'd been drugged. It felt like I had no control.

If I picked up the Bible and began to read, I would be asleep in just a few minutes. I fought it and tried to push through. Sometimes I could, and other times I could not. That is when I discovered the importance of worship music... songs to the Lord.

I remembered I was a worshipper. I had just been worshipping the wrong things. I played audio Bible readings in several rooms in my house. I prayed and worshipped in my living room for hours upon hours. At times, I felt guilty and like I needed to stop worshipping and focus on studying the Bible. But I somehow felt the Lord's presence and heard Him say it was okay and that I was doing exactly what He wanted me to do.

I could get lost in worship and lose track of time. It was a place of peace and comfort. It was a refuge for me. What a glorious place I had found! It was as if I had accidentally found it. No one had taught me to worship. I had not been to church or around believers talking about Jesus in about 20 years.

But the creature didn't stay gone. It returned repeatedly, and each time I told it to leave, it left. Jesus was teaching me my authority in Him. I hadn't picked up a Bible yet and didn't know Scripture, but He told me, *"I have given you authority to trample snakes and scorpions, and over all the power of the enemy; nothing by any means shall hurt you."* I Googled it. To my surprise, it was in the Bible—Luke 10:19!

I started reading my Bible to see what God had said and might be saying. Many supernatural things were happening at this time. I went to bed with my Bible, and though I would try to read it, I would quickly fall asleep. I just wanted my Bible close to me; even though there was no supernatural power in the physical presence of the Bible, it comforted me.

The enemy did *not* like it. One night I awoke to my Bible flying off the bed. When I picked it up, I noticed claw marks had ripped through the pages.

For the next several months, Jesus showed up every night. He would softly speak to me. Sometimes I would remember what He had said. At other times, I simply sat peacefully at His feet, not paying full attention. Perhaps you wonder how I could not have paid full attention to what He was saying. I was so comfortable soaking in His presence; He was all that was on my mind. I was at complete peace in His presence, and I was desperate for peace and rest.

Once, when I was sitting at His feet, not focusing on what He was saying, He began describing future events that seemed quite profound. I sat up and said aloud to Him, "Oh, let me pay attention to what you are saying about my son." He laughed and said, "This is not for your son, this is for you."

I grew up in church, from around five or six years old. A sweet elderly couple, Mr. and Mrs. Bates, would pick us up every Sunday and take us to church. They were instrumental in building a spiritual foundation and introducing my sisters and me to Jesus. Our parents didn't attend church at that time, but the Bates made sure we were there at every opportunity.

This church's pastor was a wonderful pastor and preacher. He was kind and made everyone he met feel valuable and important to him. I do not know how he did it, but he did. It was a gift from God, and he did not squander his gift. However, religion and religious beliefs became a weapon with a lot of rules and regulations. Threats of going to hell became a tool the enemy used to keep me from seeing God as a loving parent and a loving God.

During nighttime thunderstorms, I would experience fear and trembling, thinking the Lord was coming back right then and I would surely be going to hell. It was difficult for me to see a loving, good, gracious God when I was hearing the "hell, fire and damnation" version.

There were events in my life that betrayed my trust in men. As I grew to learn about sin, I became consumed with guilt. Not knowing better, I took responsibility for any of their acts against me. It didn't help that the enemy engrained in me that I was shameful.

So, shame became a large part of my identity. How does a small girl deal with issues of abuse when others either ignore the fact that it's occurred or blame her for it? I was clearly the problem. It was me who was dirty. I was the unworthy one who became hopeless.

As a result, as I sat in church and heard the sermons, I heard the sermons through tainted ears and saw their truths through myopic eyes. I believed in God. I knew He had standards. But it was clear that I would never be able to live up to the standards that were being preached. Grace? Grace was never a consideration. It was all my fault.

As I got older, I looked for other viewpoints and ways out of what caused me so much anxiety, worry and fear. In my mind, I could not reconcile that I would spend eternity in hell. I was trapped. How could I get out of this predicament? There had to be another way.

OTHER WAYS

In college, I was introduced to alternative ways of thinking. I was being told there was no hell. There was nothing to fear. At first, it was a gradual transition that became a force and eventually became all-consuming. The introduction of chakras, meditation, crystals, auras, Reiki and reincarnation became a fascination.

I spent hours upon hours studying and learning all I could about healing as I searched for ways to heal the ever-present brokenness gnawing at me. After all, this is a big world. There had to be other ways to find peace. Maybe this technique or that one would work, and I would be healed. Maybe this new oil or crystal would take away the pain. One year led to the next, and for 20 years, I looked for inner healing in all the wrong places.

In the process, I discovered I was rather intuitive. I could often sense things about others without them telling me. I

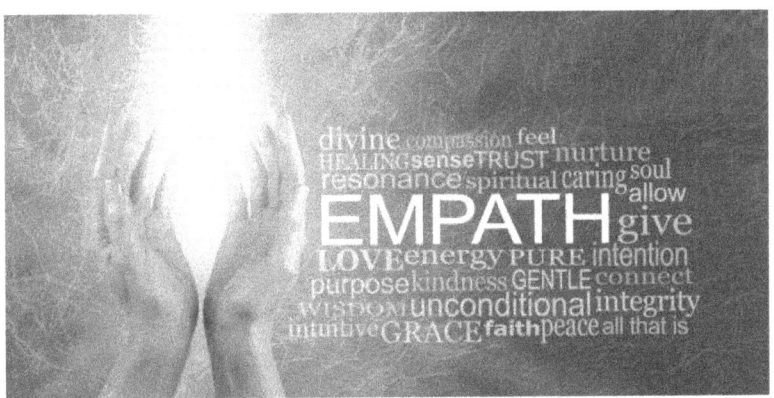

could "feel" what they were feeling at a deep level. It made continually being around people quite exhausting. This was a great set-up by the enemy to isolate me from others. It also set me up for New Age beliefs. Because I was empathetic and full of mercy, I began being referred to as an "Empath." I was special and becoming more special as I delved deeper into it.

I was called to heal others. Why else would the Universe (what I called God) give me the ability to feel what others felt, if not to "heal" them? I had discovered my purpose. There was no way to turn this off, nowhere to take it, except upon myself to be "a savior" to those who needed saving. To me, I was no longer the problem. I was part of the solution! I also discovered the more I used my gift, the better I became at it.

When I would share what I was feeling, especially with a troubled soul, it excited me to see their surprise, seeing that someone else knew and understood them. They were typically quite thankful. And I liked trying to "fix" people. It allowed me to focus on others and not consider how I might need to heal or grow. Or even that I might be wrong. Frankly, I loved the affirmation and adoration I received, and I felt personally powerful with this gift.

Early on, I adopted the belief that crystals had healing powers. Certain crystals, I believed, held power to penetrate the heart (chakra), clear the lungs (chakra), or open the third eye (wisdom) to see the unseen. Knowing the future. Knowing the past. Or just knowing. The more I searched and researched, the more this new world drew me in. It was intoxicating and exhilarating.

This New Age Movement seemed to be the answer to everything. I felt so special. I had longed to feel special, to be important, to not be discarded. With this kind of knowledge and power and my gift of empathy, I would not be so easy to discard. I began to spiritualize everything and looked for opportunities to share my knowledge. I relished every opportunity to show others what I knew about them. After all, I was an *Empath*. I was non-judgmental, and they were okay, just as they were.

At the same time, I also became weirder and weirder to my family and some friends.

THE HAND OF GOD PROTECTING ME

As I dove deeper into what I would later discover was witchcraft, my sister was drawn deeper into drug addiction and all that it entailed.

My sister was so oppressed by her demons that she would speak non-stop to what appeared to most of us to be nothing. There was no one there, at least no one we could see. She constantly talked, and we could hardly get a word in edgewise. In fact, she had only seconds of lucidity at a time. It was heartbreaking to see her in this shape. No one in this world could help her.

At this time, she was homeless, so our parents bought her a travel trailer and got her set up so she would always have a home base. But she was so far out there that it was difficult to be around her. However, I was still concerned about her and would go at least once a month to ensure she had food.

On one occasion, I asked a friend from church to go with me because I did not feel safe being with her completely alone. I should have known this day she was in a bad way because when I got there to pick her up, she grabbed me by my hair and pulled me to the floor.

Then when we got in the car and I was trying to take her to get food, she pulled a box cutter out of her purse and threatened to kill me if I didn't take her to her drug dealers house. I had no intention of taking her to his house and prayed quickly, "Jesus." He instantly put into my mind to tell her I wanted to get a sandwich first, then I would take her.

I told her I wanted to get a sandwich and a coke, and she agreed we could stop at a convenience store. I turned to my friend and whispered as I was getting out of the car, call the police. My friend called the police and I planned to stall in getting my sandwich until the police arrived. I was able to mention to the sandwich maker to make my sandwich very slow as my sister had threatened to kill me, and we had called the police.

I am not sure the sandwich maker heard or understood me, but the Lord protected me, and the sandwich was slowly made. While I waited for the police, my sister stood beside me, with her hand on the box cutter, opened in her purse, as if to threaten me.

The police arrived, handcuffed her, and put her in the patrol car while they took my statement. They also searched my car and then took her to jail. When I got back in my car, my phone was nowhere to be found. I could not believe she had taken my phone, but she had. She had thought about this and what she wanted that day. I stopped by the jail, and sure enough, they had it in the things they had taken from her. I am so grateful the Lord protected me.

He has protected me many times. Some I am aware of, and others I may never know about.

Chapter 2

Nothing New About the New Age Movement

Most of us today are familiar with the term "New Age." But as I became involved with it, I found the "New Age Movement" to be a bit complex and difficult to define. It was a catchall phrase for 'spiritual' but not 'religious' people.

Because I was undoubtedly spiritual and wanted nothing to do with religion or Jesus, at least not the Jesus I had in mind. And yet, I would have told you I was a Christian. Throughout this book, I will use "New Age" as an umbrella term to describe a diverse group of people who generally accept similar metaphysical beliefs and practices. Although there is no set list of these, there are some common themes.

The New Age Movement, which in many ways is a pseudo-religion, is often referred to as a cult. Curious westerners are often fascinated by the philosophies and religions of other countries and cultures. It appeals to them because, in many cases, it is their first consideration of spiritual experiences. They see them as possible paths to enlightenment. Many people discover New Age philosophies when they become vegans (vegetarians).

However, after my encounter with the real Jesus, I came to realize that New Age is quite deceptive. It is filled with outright lies and half-truths and often proposes things without evidence. It makes promises it does not keep. Worse still, in many aspects, it is Satanic. I say that because some of the practices in the New Age community are also practiced by Satanists. Through the New Age Movement, Satan plays on our deepest longings for peace, spirituality, connection, abundance and immortality.

It makes one feel "woke," which is the current term for actively aware and attentive to important facts and issues of social injustice. Some estimates are that as many as 50% of Americans, including many of those who consider themselves Christian, hold to at least one New Age belief. Although a fringe movement 50 years ago, in many ways it has become mainstream today. However, as I hope to point out, the New Age stream is polluted.

One common belief among New Agers is of a coming new age, a utopian age of harmony and enlightenment, sometimes referred to as "the age of Aquarius." This new age is expected to be one of light and love, with heightened spiritual consciousness, which will usher in an eradication of hunger, poverty, sickness/disease, racism, sexism and war. Adherents believe they can experience a foretaste of the coming enlightenment through personal spiritual transformation, inner healing and growth.

Though referred to as "new," as I will point out, the New Age Movement does not represent radical new concepts at all. It is merely a collection of ancient spiritual beliefs and practices. Most can be traced to Eastern religions like Hinduism, Buddhism, Taoism and other ancient traditions. All of them are contrary to biblical Christianity and the teachings of Jesus. And how could I not tell you about Him? Did you read my testimony?

Chapter 3

The Modern Roots of the Movement

Some claim the New Age Movement was born out of the secular progressivism of the 1950s. While it is true that attention has been focused on it since the 1950s-1980s, most of the beliefs and practices involved have been around in one form or another since the 2nd Century. It surfaced mainly in the United States and Britain in the 1960s and 1970s.

In the 1970s, the belief in the power of spirituality spread through the occult and metaphysical religious communities, as practitioners began to focus on personal spiritual transformation. You may recall or have read about when in 1968 John Lennon and George Harrison, members of the famed musical group *The Beatles,* visited India in search of spiritual enlightenment from the Maharishi Mahesh Yogi. Lennon eventually rejected the Maharishi, but Harrison remained a religious devotee for the rest of his life.

Today there are many New Age groups, many with their own books, seminars and periodicals, each claiming to be the most effective way to reconnect with nature, develop mind, body and spirit, and realize one's personal divinity. That is right. As universalists, they believe God is in all things and all people. It is Pantheism, the belief that all of reality, and everything in it, *is* God. One example of this is their belief in "the divine-human spirit," in other words that we are all gods.

These New Age groups vary according to their chosen occult practices, among which are psychic readings, Yoga, transcendental meditation, Tarot cards, astrology, past life regression, metaphysical teaching sessions, and more. Other groups focus on such things as natural healing practices, acupuncture, herbal therapy, natural foods and spiritual healing techniques.

I tried them all. I was searching for healing, knowing I needed it, and desperately looked anywhere to find it. I was unaware that Jesus provided it. I had no idea how to get it, even being in church. I am not sure if it was not taught or if my jaded perception and demonic influences just blocked my ability to see and hear the truth.

Most New Agers not only believe in spirit beings, but they also seek guidance and knowledge of the future from them via channeling, Ouija Board, psychics, tea leaves, etc. Most also believe that heavenly bodies (the sun, moon and stars) influence the affairs of humanity; thus, the practice of astrology.

As for me, I wanted to know the future so I could prepare and protect myself. I was so filled with fear that I felt knowing the future might mitigate the fear factor in my life. However, there was never enough knowledge or reassurance, and one revelation led to seeking another.

Chapter 4

Who Is God to New Agers?

Though some New Age practitioners refer to themselves as Christians, they generally reject traditional Christianity. Why? It is mainly because the Christian faith is based on God's will and His Word. However, the New Age Movement is centered on every person's autonomy (free will), relativism, and spiritualism.

They accept the concept of evil and separation from God, although they do not believe in the God of the Bible. Instead, they believe that God is all things and in all people. According to them, each of us has forgotten our innate divinity, which is the true essence of the universe.

The answer to this dilemma is to awaken the divine within us. To achieve this, they use practices like meditation, breathing exercises, hypnotism, yoga, diet, crystals and spirit guides. It seems that all these practices have one common goal: to awaken the god within.

Not being followers of the Bible, much of what they teach and accept, though religious sounding, is contrary to biblical teaching. One example of this is their view of Jesus Christ. They respect Jesus historically as a teacher but not as the Savior of the world, Son of God, or a third part of the Trinity. Since they reject Jesus as God and believe they are divine, they see no need for the Christian gospel.

The New Age Movement aims to promote its brand of spirituality. Some call it "the Aquarian Conspiracy." For example, New Age adherents view reincarnation as an ascension process through which each person identifies and works to correct their unresolved issues, living life after life. This was such a relief to me to know that I had multiple chances and multiple opportunities to "get it right."

Not surprisingly, that concept is incompatible with Scripture, which says, *"... people are destined to die once, and after that, to face judgment."* (Hebrews 9:27, NIV) The Bible warns us to beware of false prophets and teachers, and New Age proponents are not exceptions. I had no concept of grace and forgiveness or that we become new creations when we are born again. Because of my works-mentality and perfectionistic drive, I knew I would never be good enough. Therefore, my only hope was to live multiple lives and "re-dos."

While the movement has its share of followers, as I've said, it is not a unified ideology. It is a loose, irrational social movement with members from a wide variety of backgrounds and beliefs. The goal of the New Age Movement is to transcend existing religions and create a global religion, though they would not likely use the word "religion."

Having been around for decades, with the help of the Internet, thousands of books, and hundreds of periodicals, the New Age has expanded into various sub-sects.

To a true Christian, God is *not* a higher power. He is the *Highest Power!* Even Satan refers to Him as the Most High. He said, *"I will ascend above the tops of the clouds; I will make myself like the Most High."* (Isaiah 14:14)

New Agers commonly call God "the Universe." I discovered God is *not* the universe. He created the universe! The Bible teaches, *"For in Him (Christ) all things were created, things in heaven and on earth, visible and invisible, whether thrones or dominions or rulers or authorities. All things were created through Him and for Him. He is before all things, and in Him all things hold together."* (Colossians 1:16-17)

Chapter 5

What Attracts People to New Age?

There are many reasons why people are drawn into the New Age Movement. Some are merely looking for something to relieve their boredom. Others are looking for ways to find peace of mind, resolve guilt, or find their life's purpose. Some are fascinated with the mysterious, and many are simply influenced by their friends. Some have left Christianity because of the lack of power seen in the church and not knowing how to reconcile their spiritual void other than looking for other things that seem to have more power.

A friend of mine was the pastor of a church in Houston several years ago when a local high school principal called him to ask a probing question. "Reverend," he said. "We are finding a rising number of our students involved in witchcraft and satanism. Can you explain why that may be?"

The pastor asked the principal, "Sir, do you attend church regularly?"

"Yes, my family and I do,"

"Do you routinely see examples of God's power demonstrated in the church you attend?"

"No, Reverend, I can't say I have," the principal replied.

The pastor continued, "Sir, I suspect your students are seeking demonstrations of spiritual power."

A principle thing I'll mention several times in the pages that follow is this: *There are ONLY TWO sources of spiritual power. They are God and Satan.* To know the difference often takes spiritual discernment and wisdom. Why? It can be like the difference between gold and fool's gold. Jesus said in Matthew 24:24 that a day will come when many will be deceived.

When one is only taught book knowledge but doesn't see any real changes or manifestations of new life, it is easy to look elsewhere. And there is no lack of power being promoted by New Agers. New Agers believe in a spirit world and in the power of that world. They talk about it, write about it, promote it, and live it. I was deceived into believing any power I saw was godly. However, I came to find out, not all spiritual power is good or godly.

Each of us faces challenging life experiences at times. Some begin at a very young age, as was in my case. Others experience them later in life. When those challenges leave us wounded, we often begin to search for solutions. New Agers tend to promote their pet procedures as "cure-alls." However, we should remember that what benefits one individual may be of little or no benefit to another. And if the power involved is not God's power, the end can be more than disappointing. It can be disastrous.

So, whether it is a physical challenge, financial, relational, or other, without a strong foundation, many turn to New Age for help. Let's consider then some of the primary attractants.

Chapter 6
A Desire to Know the Future

Everyone wants a sense of purpose, guidance and direction. How else can we measure our gains and losses... our progress? One of the most successful books of our time is Rick Warren's *Purpose Driven Life*. Everyone wants to know their purpose. New Age doctrines and activities entice some who lack a sense of direction and are seeking their reason for being.

Several New Age practices offer to provide life direction. Insecure individuals find a degree of comfort in being validated. New Age validates your gifts and talents and you as a person. Individuals looking for validation find a degree of comfort in searching for their purpose, and for that matter, each of us has a purpose.

TAROT CARDS

I was specifically involved with Tarot Card readings as I looked for answers and ways to validate what I was thinking or hearing/feeling, but also really wanted to 'know what was coming' as I had such a fear of the unknown, I was looking for ways to 'know', to help mitigate being blindsided as I had previously been in several situations. I wanted the "control" it brought. After I came to Jesus, I was shocked that what I had been practicing in New Age was witchcraft and an abomination to God.

"What are Tarot Cards?" you may be asking. Tarot cards are decks of cards that have been used throughout Europe since the mid-15th century. Several games based on tarot use them, including the French Tarot, the Italian Tarocchini and the Austrian Kingrufen. Various versions of these games are still played today and are considered by many an excellent source of inspiration and information.

Tarot cards have a long history. They were initially used as a parlor game. Although the first recorded decks are dated from various areas of Italy, they were not used for divination until the 18th century. There are many ways to interpret the meaning of tarot cards, and anyone can learn "the art" of reading them.

The major arcana consists of 21 cards and two minor arcana, which are the two most common types of Tarot decks. Each of these cards has its own meaning and can help you understand the situation you are in. Practitioners promise the more you know about the tarot cards, the more you'll be able to get your life back on track.

Tarot cards can be used for several purposes and often serve as divination tools. Tarot card readers claim to provide clients insight into their financial, love, and family life. Each reader uses their style and method of divination.

Some New Age practitioners believe the cards will help them achieve a spiritual vision. However, it is not true. The occult is a non-Christian concept, and therefore a New Age false religion. To practice the Tarot, one needs to be religious. I became involved with Tarot cards through a friend who took me to a professional psychic in Austin. This guy shuffled cards and read my future and told me all about my past.

He also read my palm and told me about my past lives. I wanted to know the future, usually about my love life, to preempt whatever was going to come my way and knock me down. If I knew what was going to happen beforehand, I could be prepared and in control. I liked being in control and thus preventing any future hurt. Relationships were also one of my gods. Being in a relationship meant I was valued, and it was drug-like.

Others want general hidden knowledge. They seek supernatural guidance by consulting the Ouija Board.

OUIJA BOARD

Some refer to the Ouija Board as a talking board, a spirit board, or a witch's board. It is a flat board with the letters of the alphabet on it. The board is sold as a popular game for children and teenagers. During a seance, participants place their fingers on the pointer, which often moves mysteriously from letter to letter to answer questions. Created in the mid-1800s, it is still popular today.

The Ouija Board has a long, dark history. The original version was used to communicate with the spirits of the deceased, or so they thought. It has been a mainstay of horror movies for decades, and it is not surprising that the popularity of this paranormal tool is soaring. Hundreds of movies have featured the Ouija Board. The most famous are: *The Uninvited* (1944), *The Exorcist* (1973), and *The Changeling* (1980).

In actuality, the Ouija Board is an occult tool, used to channel spirits (demons), which masquerade as spirits of the deceased. The activity is supposed to end when the user says goodbye. However, there are many stories of people who were possessed by demons through involvement with the Ouija board.

The movie *The Uninvited* depicts the Ouija board as an entry point for possession. In the movie, a family holds a seance to inquire about death. Deliverance ministers often encounter those who became demonized because of their involvement with the board say that the Ouija Board is one of the fastest ways for a person to become demonized, commonly called "demon-possessed."

A young high school girl reported to her pastor that she and three others seemed to be getting answers from the spirit world to their questions one night. At one point, they asked the Board, "How far does your power reach?" The Board spelled out, "T.O. T.H.E. B.L.O.O.D.;" a reference to Christ and the blood He shed at Calvary.

Parents, grandparents, aunts, uncles and friends. I implore you to not take this lightly. A Ouija Board is not a toy. It is a gateway, an opening into something you do NOT want to get into. One thing leads to another. It does. Please take heed. It is not a joke, and I am not overreacting in telling you this.

Although I did not play with it much, I was exposed to it several times. Once by a neighbor and another by a cousin. This brings up the subject of family lineage and generational curses. If you or a family member have been involved, Jesus gave us a new covenant. We can confess our sins and the sins of our forefathers and break curses. We can repent and refuse to participate further.

Hopefully, you understand that the Ouija Board is not a toy, is dangerous, and should never be in your home or among your possessions. One of the most prominent ways people use in search of their future is astrology. For decades, major newspapers have included daily horoscope readings. Those readings are also found online.

ASTROLOGY

Millions of people don't start their day until they have first checked their horoscope. I was one of those. What is astrology? Some confused astronomy with astrology. Astronomy is the scientific study of the stars and planets. Astrology, however, is a pseudoscience not based on truth.

Astrology is an ancient belief system based on the movement and relative positions of the stars and planets from which practitioners claim to deduce information about earthly events to come. And oddly, it is believed that one's birth month determines their character traits and personality. However, astrology is filled with myths.

The Zodiac, influenced by Taoism, is a chart depicting the heavenly bodies, based on the Chinese calendar. In the Zodiac, are 12 calendar divisions, called birth signs. They are Aries, Taurus, Gemini, Cancer, Leo, Virgo, Libra, Scorpio, Sagittarius, Capricorn, Aquarius and Pisces. Each is represented by a Greek symbol, dating back to the Middle Ages.

Would anyone suppose astrology holds true for birds, plants and animals? Of course not. That's absurd. Why can't astrology apply to other living beings? It's simply impossible that the positions of stars and planets act on *only* human beings!

Most importantly, however, astrology is not based on science but is a flawed argument based on personal beliefs unsupported by evidence. The actual planets, as they orbit the sun, change position and wander about. Adherents of astrology claim to use their movement to understand their personalities and, to some extent, control their destinies.

The days of our lives are not determined by the position of the heavenly bodies. The Psalmist wrote in the biblical book of Psalms:

"My frame was not hidden from you
when I was made in the secret place
when I was woven together in the depths of the earth.
Your eyes saw my unformed body;
all the days ordained for me were written in your book
before one of them came to be.
How precious to me are your thoughts, God!
How vast is the sum of them!"
(Psalm 139:15-17)

You and I are not accidents. God purposefully created us and has charted a path for each of our lives. To know that path, we must first get to know Him. Strangely, some people invite spirit beings into their bodies to access the supernatural! They are referred to as "channels."

CHANNELING

Channeling is another way of looking for guidance and unknown knowledge. What is channeling? It is considered a method of communication with what New Agers refer to as "high-level spirit-teachers." However, they are not "high level" at all. They are merely run-of-the-mill ground-level demons masquerading. They often even masquerade as one's departed loved ones. The spirits communicate through the "channel."

You are not speaking to your loved one. I know you may have found comfort in believing so, and this may cause you

pain and sadness to believe differently, but Jesus clearly states otherwise. And believing a lie won't bring you comfort and peace in the long run.

One might consider a "channel" as a person who serves as a bridge between the natural and the supernatural, the known and the unknown. Some channels think they are connecting with other forms of consciousness, such as deceased individuals, and angels. But we'll see shortly if that isn't the case.

A client may experience different emotions during a channeling session. Some people may become excited or confused, while others may feel nervous or afraid that they're going crazy. One may even experience a higher degree of dissociation, or psychosis. While the symptoms of channeling are not always pathological, they can be frightening for some. Scientists, who disbelieve in the supernatural, are skeptical about channeling's legitimacy. They believe the messages aren't "from beyond" but are only manifestations of the channeler's psyche.

New Agers generally consider channeling to be a safe and effective method for connecting with angels. These spirits are said to be powerful, but they are not necessarily evil. True. Angels are not evil. But when one seeks spirit communication, they have no assurance of what is responding to them. Demons are great pretenders.

There is a fad of worshipping angels. We are to worship only our Creator, God. There are even some Christian leaders who wrongly teach how to command angels to do one's bidding. Angels are exclusively God's to command. They are not subject to our prayers, our directions, or our desires. Never in one of the nearly 300 times angels are mentioned in Scripture is anyone praying *to* or calling *on* one for help, and there is absolutely nothing of one commanding angel at all.

Angels appeared to people on many occasions in the biblical record, but not because people sought them out. God dispatched them.

Here is the Apostle Paul's warning in Colossians 2:18. "*Let no man beguile you... [into] worshipping angels, intruding into those things which he hath not seen, vainly puffed up by his fleshly mind.*"

I know many people who also believe that their loved one comes back as an angel, their angel, that watches over them. Nowhere in Scripture does it say this. This is a dangerous belief. I know that some want to believe their loved one is still around them on earth but they aren't. But you can have the assurance you will see them again if you and they are born again. *(See the end of the book for more details.)*

Does the practice of channeling appear in the Bible? The Bible clearly states that evil spirits exist and that a possessed host will tell mixed fortunes. Therefore, the Bible cautions against spiritism, divination, and other practices that seek to communicate with spirit guides and other entities.

PSYCHICS & FORTUNE TELLERS

In the New Age arena, there are generally two types of fortune tellers and psychics. There are the *predictive* and the *guidance-based*. The former is believed to predict the future, while the latter helps their clients understand their present circumstances, resolve problems, and provide direction.

Guidance-based practitioners may also be referred to as *esoteric practitioners*. They do not predict the future but instead attempt to help clients improve their lives.

Fortune tellers are known by many titles, such as soothsayers, prophets, clairvoyants, sibyls or psychics. They use techniques like crystallomancy, palmistry, cartomancy, tasseography, reading tea leaves or Tarot Cards, and astromancy to make predictions. Despite the negative connotations, some people still seek them out.

There are no official regulations for psychic services, and many aspiring "psychics" prey on the gullible for financial gain. Relationship readings are the most common. These are typically used to get assurances and guidance in relationships. Unlike other types of psychics, love-related readings can be expensive.

In Acts 16:16-18 (ISV), we read where Paul and Silas encountered a young lady who told fortunes. They wrote,

"*Once, as we were going to the place of prayer, we met a slave girl who had a spirit of fortune-telling and who had*

brought her owners a great deal of money by predicting the future. She would follow Paul and us and shout, 'These men are servants of the Most High God and are proclaiming to you a way of salvation!'

"She kept doing this for many days until Paul became annoyed, turned to her, and told the spirit, 'I command you in the name of Jesus the Messiah to come out of her!' And it came out that very moment."

WHAT GOD SAYS

God forbids our seeking help from fortune tellers and psychics. In Deuteronomy 18:9-13 (TLB), we read: *"When you arrive in the Promised Land you must be very careful lest you be corrupted by the horrible customs of the nations now living there. For example, an Israeli who presents his child to be burned to death as a sacrifice to heathen gods must be killed. No one may practice black magic, call on the evil spirits for aid, be a fortune teller, be a serpent charmer, medium or wizard, or call forth the spirits of the dead. Anyone doing these things is an object of horror and disgust to the Lord, and it is because the nations do these things that the Lord your God will displace them. You must walk blamelessly before the Lord your God."*

God alone knows the future. In Isaiah 8:19 (TLB), we read: *"So why are you trying to find out the future by consulting witches and mediums? Don't listen to their whisperings and mutterings. Can the living find out the future from the dead? Why not ask your God?"*

Why don't people seek God for future knowledge? Because God has His mind and will. He won't be manipulated by, or be subservient to, man. His revelations, which are many, are given when, where, and to whom He chooses. Withholding such info keeps us trusting Him, which is why He forbids our seeking knowledge from beyond. He is jealous for our trust. The Bible instructs that *"He is a jealous God."* (Deuteronomy 4:24)

There are gifts the Holy Spirit gives, like prophecy. He gives these gifts without repentance, and some involved in the New Age like I was, have this gift. However, they have accessed the wrong spirit. This person is gifted by God to discern and hear/see what *He is saying*; however, it is by the Holy Spirit and not just any spirit.

There is a difference. If we utilize this gift apart from God, we are operating in the wrong spirit. He can deliver us, but if we are not in the Word of God and tuned into Him, we will be tuned to the wrong spirit.

So, how do we tune into the right spirit? More of this is to come in the following chapters.

Chapter 7

A Desire to Know the Past

Just as some are drawn in with a desire to know their future, others long to know their past. With reincarnation, people want to know about past lives they believe they have lived.

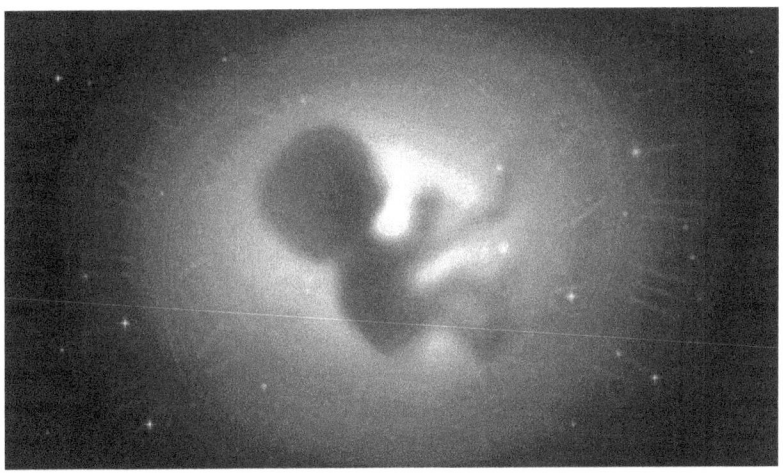

REINCARNATION

Reincarnation is the belief that after death, the non-physical essence of a person (their human soul) begins a new life in a different physical form. Reincarnation is sometimes referred to as transmigration or rebirth (not the same as being born again, as Christ taught). However, there are some myths and misconceptions surrounding reincarnation.

According to the Hindu tradition, reincarnation occurs when the soul is reborn in a new body. However, according to Scripture, each new body is an entirely different person and has not previously lived. We die once and are then judged by God.

This caused me so much anxiety and caused me to look for other beliefs that gave me multiple chances to live again. It was important to me to have multiple chances because I knew I could never be good enough to die once and then be judged. If I had multiple opportunities, surely, I could get it right. Surely, I could eventually reach perfection.

The notion of reincarnation is, of course, a controversial concept. The vast majority of Western Christians reject it outright. However, reincarnation is a mystical concept that has become popular in Western culture, especially as it relates to the New Age Movement.

Some believe their past lives *can* and *should* be remembered. Some say they have "dreamed" about their past lives, while others believe they have been "reincarnated" many times and lived many lifetimes. Some believe their souls are in a constant state of flux, and they are constantly in transition. This belief is central to many New Age communities.

Reincarnation is a common belief in many cultures and an important tenet of Indian religions. Reincarnation is also commonly believed in various tribal societies around the world. The concept of reincarnation is common in some cultures, including Buddhism and Hinduism.

WHAT DOES THE BIBLE SAY ABOUT REINCARNATION?

As I mentioned, reincarnation is strongly opposed by most Christians, as it compromises several fundamental tenets of the Christian faith. It teaches that we have multiple lifetimes in which we can cleanse our souls of sin as we live one life after another. Scripture teaches in Hebrews 9:27 that *"man is appointed ONCE to die and after that, the judgment."*

I can see how one might confuse the dozen or more resurrections from the dead that are mentioned in the Bible, in addition to Christ's resurrection, with reincarnation. A resurrected person, on the other hand, is the same person revived to continue their same life. One is a lifetime after lifetime striving toward purity and perfection. The other is an extension of the same lifetime.

Reincarnation eliminates the need for a Savior and bases one's salvation on their good works, which directly contradicts Ephesians 2:8-9 (NIV): *"For it is by grace you have been saved, through faith—and this is not from yourselves, it is the gift of God—not by works, so that no one can boast."*

So reincarnation undermines the doctrine of atonement, forgiveness and grace, which are core components of the Christian faith. I can see why Satan would teach against this. No need for a savior when you have so many lifetimes to reach perfection, all the while becoming more and more godlike yourself.

We need not live another lifetime to work on cleansing ourselves. 1 John 1:9 tells us clearly, *"If we confess our sins, He [God] is faithful and just to forgive us our sins and to cleanse us from all unrighteousness."* Done!

Yes, some claim to have been reincarnated, some multiple times. Some New Agers, whether out of curiosity or for some other reason, undergo regressive hypnosis to investigate. This is like rebirthing, which we'll investigate next. A hypnotist puts them under a spell of sorts, then coaches them regressively back to their birth, then pre-birth, to supposedly touch base with a previous lifetime, from which they can gather "facts."

There have been many movies in which reincarnation was featured. You may recall that Hollywood actress Shirley MacLaine was a big promoter of the concept of reincarnation. Interestingly, by hearing the testimonies of their former lives, you will discover that virtually all of their previous lives ended in violent deaths.

Many women who profess to have past life memories have the same stories. "I was an Egyptian Pharaoh's daughter who was poisoned." "Then I was a Swedish fisherman's daughter who was drowned at sea." Or, "I was a Civil War nurse who was shot on the battlefield as I was giving aid to a dying soldier."

I, too, tried my hand at learning about my past lives through gurus. Of course, I was a princess or queen or some exalted person who had a tragic death, which added to my sense of being special. And don't we all want to feel loved, accepted, and special?

Also, I finally came to myself and was ready to stop living in the pain of it all and forgive and move on. People tell you forgiveness is for you, not for the other person. This was a hard thing to understand, but it is true. Forgiveness changes YOU. You don't have to keep repeatedly reliving the pain day in and day out. That is torment itself! It was torment for me.

You should also know that there are what's commonly known as "false memories." They are not memories recalled but memories implanted. And they can seem quite real. More about them to come. They are often a problem for law enforcement and legal matters, especially concerning ritual child abuse.

Simply put, God says there are no second chances to live another lifetime. (But more to come on how to be forgiven completely; with the slate wiped clean, there is hope!) We each have one life to live, and we should soberly consider what follows it.

In Luke 16:19-24, Jesus described the deaths of two men. A beggar named Lazarus and the rich man from whom he begged. *"So it was that the beggar (Lazarus) died and was carried by the angels to Abraham's bosom. (Heaven) The rich man also died and was buried. And being in torment in Hades (Hell), he lifted up his eyes and saw Abraham afar off and Lazarus in his bosom. Then he cried and said, 'Father Abraham, have mercy on me, and send Lazarus that he may dip the tip of his finger in water and cool my tongue; for I am tormented in this flame.'"*

In 2 Corinthians 5:8, God says of a believer, *"To be absent from the body is to be present with the Lord."*

REBIRTHING

You exited your mother's womb and came into this world in a rather abrupt and traumatic fashion. Whether you entered naturally, with the help of forceps, or by Caesarian section, you left a warm, soft, safe, dark environment and likely burst into a harsh, brightly lit, confusing world.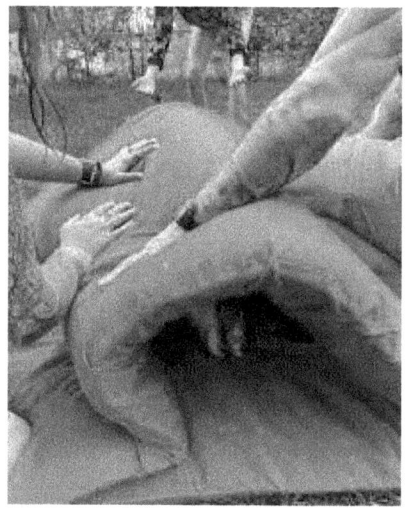

The elements of your birth set into motion many things about life and how you will handle it. Rebirthing, a New Age practice, is a regressive hypnosis procedure made popular in the 1970s, which involves continuous breathing and the analysis of family dynamics from your conception to birth.

The practice is often compared to those of the ancient Greeks, including ecstasy. Practitioners claim that rebirthing is like being reincarnated. It's an attempt to "relive" one's birth by simulating a return to their mother's womb and "reliving" their birth experience—thus "*re*-birthing."

For realism, some practitioners use bright lights, play heartbeat rhythmic audio loops, wrap their clients in blankets and pillows, and other elements to help recreate their subject's birth experience.

One practitioner said that experiencing his simulated birth was "like being beaten," citing many issues with childbirth.

The process typically involves a person lying in silence with their eyes closed and usually begins very relaxing. During the procedure, some may experience cramping or twitching after the session, and some people can experience extreme pain and traumatic memories during one. It's certainly not a cure-all.

Rebirthing sessions typically last approximately 90 minutes. It's a form of breathwork that supposedly helps clear destructive and negative patterns. The practitioner simulates birth in an enclosed space, like a bathtub or a hot tub. In some cases, this session takes place underwater. It is sometimes a treatment for Reactive Attachment Disorder (RAD) and anxiety.

Some alternative medicine practitioners have training in nursing and CPR, and they must be able to provide emergency care. The rebirthing experience is far from safe. It's currently outlawed in North Carolina and Colorado. A 10-year-old Colorado girl died after a 70-minute session in which she was bound with pillows to simulate the birth canal, and therapists pushed her from side-to-side to simulate contractions. There is no scientific evidence to support the practice, so rebirthing has as many opponents as proponents.

A Christian counselor I know was ministering to a young lady who had been cut off from her parents for eight years. There was no communication at all. Her parents didn't know if she was dead or alive. Why?

Because in her New Age-related rebirthing experience, she had "retrieved" memories of her father molesting her at an early age. She had confronted him, but he denied it. Her mother tried to convince her that she was mistaken. But she swore that she would never speak to him again. It had been eight long years of separation.

Her counselor sensed that her memories were not recalled but possibly implanted. A trained prayer team met with her. They prayed God would reveal the truth to her, whatever it was. Jesus said in John 16:33a that His Spirit would guide us into all truth.

At one point, as they prayed God would expose the lies and establish the truth, to everyone's surprise, she shrieked, "My Daddy didn't do this. It was all a lie."

As the ministry session concluded, she made the long-distance call to speak to her parents. She wept and apologized to them. They forgave her, and two weeks later, they spent their first Christmas together in eight years. Years later, she reported that those lies she'd believed about her father have never returned.

There are certainly times when remembering and resolving hurtful experiences is helpful. However, I believe that the ability to forget is, sometimes, as much a gift of God as the ability to remember. There are things it's better to forget, like the pain of losing a loved one or a medical procedure like childbirth or an amputation.

Some Christian counselors and ministers focus on helping clients recapture lost memories, looking for unresolved life issues. Others insist on allowing God, in His time, to revive past issues that need reconciliation. They would say that demonic spirits sometimes implant "false memories" and that a client's faulty subconscious can also produce them.

We all experience them from time to time. An example would be to believe you turned on the dishwasher before leaving for work, only to return home to discover you didn't. False memories often relate to traumatic experiences. Psychotherapists, who often encounter them, refer to them as the "false memory syndrome."

So much of this is going on in America right now, false memories and false realities. What a plan the enemy has for us to be a separated, hurt, and hurtful people.

"Rebirthers" believe that the regressive hypnotic experience helps them relive and reorder their lives—to relieve pain and release emotions. I had a rebirthing experience several times; it seemed once was not enough. It represented a "new" beginning and was supposed to help me in healing the broken pieces and the parts of the little girl that had been so mistreated and abused. This did not "fix" me.

IS REBIRTHING MENTIONED IN THE BIBLE?

According to New Agers, reincarnation occurs in a series of *actual physical* rebirths. Rebirthing is only a simulation of physical birth.

No, it isn't biblical. Some have pointed out that there are four basic questions with which every person will struggle. They are:
1. Where did I come from?
2. Why am I here?
3. Where am I going?
4. And how do I get there?

Scripture answers all four questions.

1. Over 100 verses of Scripture refer to God knowing us BEFORE we were born. We are not accidents. We were planned in the heart of God.
2. We are here by a divine plan to allow the risen Christ to live in us to impact the world and help others be reconciled to God.
3. We learn from Scripture that there are two eternal destinations for humanity. One is to be with God for eternity. The other, because of sin, is to be separated from God and be tormented for eternity.
4. We discover that to live eternally with God, we must be "born again." We must turn from self and sin, crown the risen Christ Lord of our lives, and invite Him to establish His kingdom in our hearts.

Reincarnation and rebirthing are cheap imitations of the real thing. The whole idea is to distract people from the truth of God and the God of the truth.

We can be reborn. But it has nothing to do with reviewing or reliving our physical birth. For you see, *true life isn't physical. True life is spiritual.* We are spiritual beings having physical experiences, not physical beings having spiritual experiences. God's Word reveals this to us, and not just this, but it tells us how we can experience a true spiritual rebirth.

You see, each of us was born wrong. We came out of the womb with a sin-nature we inherited from the first man, Adam. Think about it. No one must teach a baby to be stingy; babies must be taught to share. We don't have to teach a child how to lie; we only have to teach children to tell the truth. Why? It's because Adam and Eve's sinful nature was passed on to their children, and theirs... down to us. We each have an "Adamic nature." Sin is *natural* to us.

God loves us. He sent Jesus, His Son, to seek and save those who are lost. He does that by giving them a new nature, His nature.

He says if we believe that Jesus died in our place, in payment for our sin debt. And that three days later, He raised Jesus from the dead. And, if we confess Him as Lord of our lives, we will be saved.

The word "saved" means He will come into our hearts, forgive, cleanse us from our sins, and empower us to live righteously. At that point, having been born again, we become Children of God. He tells us that if we have His Son, we have life.

That spiritual new birth removes our guilt, shame, hurt, and pain. It resolves addictions and anything that torments us. The new life He gives us is eternal... it is Christ's life.

This is the part I was telling you about that was good news! We can be *re*-born again. So New Agers do have it partially right, only they leave out Jesus, and it is all about self instead. I have become very grateful to realize I am not that powerful, and I don't have to have it all figured out or be perfect.

Because Jesus is perfect. I just have to believe and accept it. It's a gift I just believe and receive. This is truly good news.

Chapter 8

The Mystery of New Age

Some are attracted to New Age philosophies by the mystery. We are living in a time when there is little discernment. This is particularly bad as we are challenged daily with new ideas and opportunities. The New Age Movement is filled with mysteries. Mysteries are attractive to curious people, especially if they are curious about life and have little discernment.

MYSTICISM

In the 18th and 19th centuries, traveling salespeople would ride from village to village selling "snake oil." They were commonly referred to as "snake oil salesmen." They each claimed their bottle of tonic, which contained no snake-derived substances at all, was a "cure-all." Whatever one's medical need, their product would solve it.

Of course, the truth was that it was nothing more than a bottle of mineral oil mixed with various active and inactive household herbs, spices, drugs and compounds, along with some food coloring. People would often feel better after taking it because of psychosomatic responses, and the scams continued.

New Age beliefs and practices are in some ways similar. Some folks do receive a level of temporary help. They sound promising until you begin to look behind the curtain. Then you discover they are nothing more than warmed-over ancient secrets that never offered any generation real and lasting help.

For example, many New Age beliefs and practices originated in places like India. Anyone who has visited India knows that those beliefs and practices have done little to advance their people. However, I love the people of India as God does. I pray that the country of India will have an awakening of the truth and experience Jesus and the one true living God. Many of them are coming to faith in Christ.

Recently, I visited with some Indian people who had statues of their gods to whom they offer sacrifices. Although many in India are still sacrificing today, many precious Indian people are receiving new life in Christ. What hope this has brought to them. Any advancement in India has come from the influences of Christianity and modern communications, not from transcendental meditation. Beggars and lepers line the streets of India today. Cows, animals that are revered and worshipped as gods, walk about freely, defiling the streets and sidewalks.

A friend of mine, on a visit to India, passed an idol shop. Noticing something that caught his eye, he entered the shop and found the owner sitting on the floor, carving a grotesque image from a large log he held with his feet. As he hammered and chiseled the form of a Hindu god, my friend asked him, "What god are you carving?"

The shop owner told him the god's name.

"And what is his job?" my friend asked.

"He's the god of prosperity," he replied with assurance.

"Hurry! Finish him!" my friend suddenly, excitedly, insisted.

"Why?" the man asked.

"Look out your window," my friend explained. "Your streets are lined with beggars, lepers and paupers. Finish creating your god so he can help them."

He said with that, the shop owner looked at him a bit bewildered with a look that seemed to say, *that almost makes sense.*

It seems to me that any thinking person would look anywhere but there for real solutions. Yet, curiosity and desperation cause people to do curious things.

I once had an encounter with the spirit behind the Hindu god Shiva. I worked in an office full of unhappy people who talked about me while in their cubicles around me. They saw me as an outsider with little value and were convinced I should not be there.

One day, I was talking to a supervisor who happened to be Indian. I don't recall the topic of our conversation, but as I was speaking, a guy stood up to stop me from talking. And as he did, I saw in the spirit realm Shiva coming after my tongue. All I could say was, "Jesus." When I did, that spirit leaped back and left me alone.

Sometime later, I had the opportunity to visit several Indian villages. Each had their temples for the worship of Shiva, the god of destruction, where they would offer sacrifices to seek his protection. Does he benefit the people? Many are gripped with poverty, disease and destruction. As they worship this "god," they are unwittingly binding themselves even tighter to its demonic stronghold.

A fundamental belief of New Age mysticism is that we are all spiritually divine beings (gods) who can achieve the perfect balance between our minds and our body. This concept, which is not seen as religious in nature, is the basic aim of the movement. In addition, the movement aims to bring about planetary as well as personal transformation through the manipulation of public opinion and societal structures. This is why it has gained such widespread acceptance and has become a growing phenomenon.

Another fundamental idea of New Age philosophy is that each of us is the sum of our experiences. The good and evil of life are not separate entities. The world is one, and each of us can choose his own path. The choices we make are the fruit of our illumination. We are created as divine beings, and though we are not to control others, we are to choose our own actions and destinies.

The New Age view of the world is based on the idea that we are all part of a whole, not separate from the rest of creation. As such, we are essentially one with *the divine*. (New Ager's reference to God.)

It has evolved from a belief in a personal god to a more universal one. The New Age movement focuses on Eastern religions and practices as they are considered free of what some describe as "Judeo-Christian distortions." They give a great deal of respect to ancient fertility cults and agricultural rites, and their god is neither personal nor transcendent. Rather, it is an "impersonal energy" present in the world and in all that exists. And what is their god's name? It is essentially "the Universe."

The deeper and deeper I got into New Age, the more I saw everything seemed focused on one's self. Everything was about me, what I wanted, and what benefits I could receive. Instead of my becoming more and more enlightened and mature, I was becoming more self-centered and childish.

While the New Age movement claims to integrate natural and spiritual reality, the concept is not based on the Bible. The Bible teaches that we are to seek God His way. However, the New Age Movement has many goals that are contrary to biblical teaching. Its members believe that they can reach the heavenly realm their way, but they do so at their own peril. God says, *"There is a way that appears to be right, but in the end, it leads to death."* (Proverbs 14:12, NIV)

THE BIBLE?

Scripture teaches us that God is three persons in One, a Trinity. He is Father, Son and Holy Spirit. It reveals that although God created man and woman in the Garden of Eden, they chose their way rather than His. That sin resulted in their being evicted from the Garden and left with a fallen, sinful inner nature that would require a new birth.

They would need to be born again, a spiritual rebirth which requires that they believe in their heart God's report that His Son, Jesus, was brutally sacrificed in their place as a sin offering. And that three days later, Jesus was raised from the dead and sent His Holy Spirit to live in them. Then when they submit their lives to His Lordship, God becomes central in their lives, and His Spirit empowers them to live lives that honor Him; and seals their eternal life in heaven.

Virtually none of the New Age concepts transfer to the biblical understanding of *true* spiritual life. Spiritual life, according to the Bible, is personal oneness and dependence on the Living God by His Holy Spirit. It is to worship the Creator, not the creation.

Romans 1:18-24 describes the New Age philosophy and why it's so blatantly nonbiblical. We read: *"The wrath of God is being revealed from heaven against all the godlessness and wickedness of people, who suppress the truth by their wickedness,* [**To suppress the truth is wickedness**] *since what may be known about God is plain to them because God has made it plain to them.* [20] *For since the creation of the world, God's invisible qualities—his eternal power and divine nature—have been clearly seen, being understood* from what has been made, so that people are without excuse. **[They are without excuse.]** *For although they knew God, they neither glorified him as God nor gave thanks to him, but their thinking became futile, and their foolish hearts were darkened.* ²² *Although they claimed to be wise, they became fools* ²³ *and exchanged the glory of the immortal God for images made to look like mortal human beings and birds and animals and reptiles.* **[They were given the revelation but chose otherwise, and their minds were darkened.]** *...They exchanged the truth about God for a lie and worshiped and served created things rather than the Creator—who is forever praised. Amen.* **[They believe and teach that God is not a personal, knowable God but instead exists in all things and all people.]** (Emphasis added)

As we can see, New Age ideology is contrary to Scripture. It is a mixture of multiple false religions, which are religions of false gods. Every part of it directs people away from Creator God and His Son, Jesus Christ, and to demonic powers and practices, faith in physical objects, and a focus on self.

So, the truth is, there are many and varied reasons people are attracted to the New Age Movement. Again, behind the curtain is Satan—a want-to-be God—drawing their attention from their only True Hope, which is new life, eternal life found in Jesus Christ. More on that later.

Chapter 9
New Age Healing Practices

Saddest to me is that many of those engaged in New Age grew up in evangelical churches. They attended weekly worship services and were involved in organized activities like youth groups, summer camps and Sunday school. Yet their issues were never resolved, and their questions were never answered. Some attended Christian colleges yet never found the love, joy, peace, and hope found in a personal relationship with Christ. How can this be?

In fact, it was in college that many were introduced to Eckhart Tolle's writings and others that created a curiosity for spiritual experiences outside of God's Word.

They (including me) were primed to investigate other promising spiritual pursuits. New Age offered us a smorgasbord of possibilities... all leading us further and further from the true and living God. One such area of specific interest was healing. As I mentioned earlier, being empathetic as I am, I could easily discern when someone was hurting. It was fascinating to think that I could have the tools to heal others as I pleased.

There are several New Age healing practices.

CRYSTALS

One popular tool for healing among New Agers is Crystals. The belief in the mystical healing power of crystals is an ancient practice to tap into the healing energies of "the universe" (God) and to enhance physical, mental, and spiritual well-being. As part of the New Age movement in the 1970s, crystals gained popularity among mainstream Western culture as an alternative means of healing and spirituality—one more readily attainable than meditation or

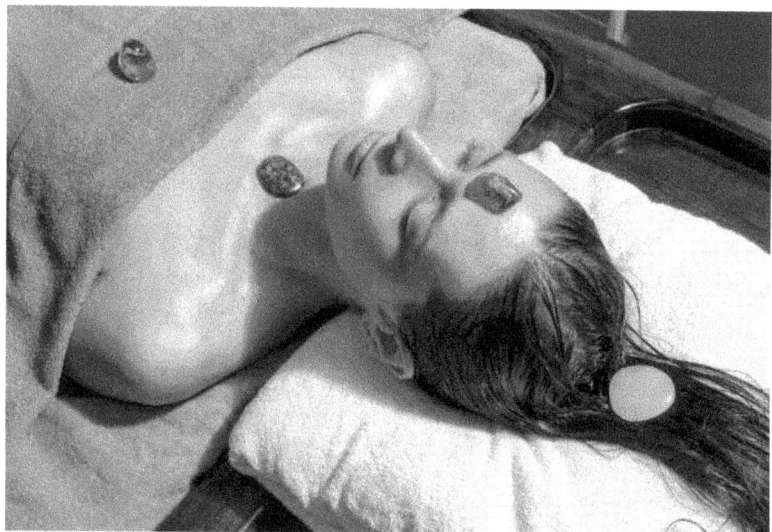

other forms of mindfulness, and that doesn't require strict religious commitment like Christianity does.

It is currently experiencing a surge in popularity in many modern societies. This trend has grown so popular that even celebrities like Victoria Beckham publicly endorse their use to promote wellness, which leads one to wonder exactly what these crystals are and why so many people believe they can help with everything from physical ailments to emotional struggles. Let's look at the phenomenon of crystal healing for a moment and find out what is behind its return to mainstream popularity today.

WHAT ARE CRYSTALS?

A crystal is an inorganic solid material that can be made into objects like jewelry or used in any number of other ways. Although sometimes referred to as rocks, they aren't rocks. They are a form of glass. Many gems are crystals, including emeralds, citrine, ruby, and sapphire. Other materials may look like crystals but don't consist entirely of ordered lattices. We see crystals every day, especially if we are wearing any kind of jewelry, but the question remains: why do New Age people believe in their use?

    The ancient Egyptians used gemstones like turquoise and lapis lazuli as healing stones. The Greeks and Romans believed in the benefits of topaz and quartz. The ancient Greeks reportedly used amethyst and hematite to decorate their holy items. The word crystal comes from the Greek word *krystallos*, meaning "coldness drawn together."

    For centuries crystals have been used by shamans (witch doctors), healers, and others in the occult community who believe them to be powerful tools to heal and protect the body and mind from negative energy. They are thought to have mystical powers that heal by drawing out negative energy and replacing it with both positive energy and healing vibrations.

    This, according to them, can be accomplished using crystal healing or therapy, which combines the use of crystals with various methods of traditional medicine to help the body heal itself from disease and injury.

Crystals are also used as tools for divination. Psychics for generations have used crystal balls to obtain hidden knowledge by occult means and spirit communication (conversing with demons), as well as in meditation exercises that help raise energy levels, creativity, and even IQ scores. Though their use had been particularly relegated to regions that use traditional healing rather than contemporary medicine, it was popularized in the New Age Movement of the 1960s and 70s through books like *Crystal Power* and *The Crystal Bible* by Judy Hall.

Something about crystals has always fascinated humans—even if we don't know why they fascinate us so much, we are drawn to them because of their beauty, allure and mystique. Some people wear crystals around their necks or carry them on keychains as good luck charms, in addition to using them to promote healing or deflect bad vibes.

AS AN ASIDE

Speaking of "good luck charms," most of us are familiar with the practice of carrying a rabbit's foot or some other object for good luck.

Among the strangest of all are gargoyles. Gargoyles are those grotesque, demonic-looking carved creatures designed by gothic architects to place on buildings. They are said to serve two purposes.

First, they often serve as downspouts to release water from the roofs of buildings. They are hollow, with an opening in the back. Rainwater flows into them from the back and flows out of their mouths rather than runs down the sides of the buildings, discoloring the stone and leaching the mortar.

Second, they are also seen perched on the ledges of buildings to ward off evil spirits. They are essentially seen as "good luck" charms. They are not created hideous looking to scare people, but rather to ward off demon spirits.

NOW BACK TO CRYSTALS

Today, this love of crystals and all they are supposed to do has only grown. Many people who have no interest in New Age beliefs or spirituality still have crystals in their homes, and some swear by their healing properties. Some doctors, who once laughed at crystal healing, now believe in the power these stones carry!

With the emergence of New Age beliefs in the 1960s, people began turning to unconventional methods to maintain good health, from holistic medicine and meditation to crystals and other New Age methods. Today's crystal healers claim that these miraculous stones, when placed on various parts of the body, can improve just about every aspect of one's health, from digestion and blood circulation to mental focus and emotional stability.

I had a massive piece of rose quartz crystal that was supposed to help heal my broken heart. It failed. I continued to look elsewhere and in other New Age practices. One thing led to the next and drew me deeper into deception. Why didn't this heal me? I was searching, I was looking, I was hurting, and I wanted to be healed!

WHAT'S WRONG WITH CRYSTALS?

There is nothing at all wrong with crystals themselves. They are beautiful expressions of God's creative handiwork. If you glance back over the preceding several paragraphs, you'll see that what people seek from crystals, they should be seeking from Jesus Christ, the healer. The Holy Spirit should be the source of man's direction and revelation. It's just another example of how the New Age directs followers away from God, and not to Him, but to self.

In the biblical Book of Revelation, the New Jerusalem (in heaven) is described as having walls of Jasper and a foundation adorned with every precious stone. From jasper to sapphire, from agate to emerald, from ruby to turquoise, and from jacinth to chrysolite. God's throne is described as crystal, and before it was what looked to be "a sea of glass." From that, it's easy to see why anyone might perceive crystals as having some form of spiritual power. It is almost as if New Age takes partial truths from the Word of God and twists them into something useful for itself. Wink, wink.

However, mature Christians will avoid adding to what the Bible clearly states and the guidance it gives. Crystals on earth have a dark background and have been used in the occult for thousands of years. We are to seek guidance from the Lord. Jesus said in John 16:13 that his Holy Spirit would guide us into *all* truth. Although healing is provided to Christ's atoning death, we should not be fooled into thinking that these beautiful stones carry the power to heal.

Let's look at another popular New Age healing method.

REIKI HEALING

The practice of Reiki healing is a subset of and is one of the oldest forms of alternative medicine. *Reiki* is a Japanese word meaning "universal life force." Again, remember, Jesus Christ said He is *"the way, the truth and the life."* (John 14:6)
Reiki practitioners use hands-on methods in attempts to transmit what they call "the universal energy" through their palms to the individual who is ill.

A typical Reiki healing treatment is simple: a practitioner sits in a chair and places their hands lightly over the client's wound or pain point. The session generally lasts no more than three to ten minutes. The hands are placed lightly over the client, and the Reiki practitioner will guide them through a process that combines the physical and spiritual aspects of Reiki. It is also a way to release emotional baggage. A trained practitioner can work with people of any age and is said to be able to help people cope with a variety of ailments.

Reiki practitioners are taught that the first step in performing Reiki healing is to ask for permission from the person they're working with. In a case like this, the practitioner can offer Reiki to a family member or friend who needs it. Some Reiki practitioners include massages in their treatment.

Reiki healing is deceptive in so many ways. It is a focused attempt to help people who truly need help. What could be wrong with that? There are even certain joys and rewards one experiences helping others. And Jesus was a healer. Aren't we commanded to do what He did?

Yes. Jesus said His followers would do the works, *even greater works* than He did. (John 14:12) The issue is not healing per se. It is the source of the power to heal. Remember our premise. There are only two sources of spiritual power in the universe. They are the power of God, our Creator, and the power of the wicked one, Satan, a created one who has chosen to usurp God. (Isaiah 14:14)

Why would Satan want someone well? Why would he provide power for someone to heal, or to be healed?

To understand that, we must understand Satan's strategies. In Isaiah 14:14, we learn that he wants to be like "the Most High God." He had been a type of angel in heaven before he rebelled against God and was cast into the earth. He is jealous of the Most High God. Interesting, isn't it, that he calls Creator God "the Most High." Note: Some declare Satan to have been an archangel. Scripture doesn't.

How you have fallen from heaven, O Lucifer, son of the dawn. You have been cast down to the earth, you who once laid low the nations. You said in your heart, "I will ascend to heaven. I will raise my throne above the stars of God. I will sit enthroned on the mount of the assembly, on the uttermost heights of the sacred mountain. I will ascend above the tops of the mountains. I will make myself like the Most High" (Isaiah 14:12-14).

Satan, who was envious of God's glory and power, declared five "I wills" in his manifesto:

1. I will ascend to heaven.
2. I will raise my throne above the stars of God.
3. I will sit enthroned on the mount of the assembly, on the utmost heights of the sacred mountain.
4. I will ascend above the tops of the clouds.
5. I will make myself like the Most High.

A mere fallen creation of God, Satan was so blinded by proud ambition and a prideful sense of self-importance and envy that he dared to rebel against the Most High. *"This is what the Lord says—Israel's King and Redeemer, the Lord Almighty: I am the first and I am the last; apart from me there is no God"* (Isaiah 44:6).

Most Christians don't believe Satan can or does heal. They forget that Jesus warned concerning the great judgment day, *"Not everyone who says to Me, 'Lord, Lord,' will enter the kingdom of heaven, but only he who does the will of My Father in heaven. Many will say to Me on that day, 'Lord, Lord, did we not prophesy in your name, and in Your name drive out demons and perform many miracles?' Then I will tell them plainly, 'I never knew you....'"* (Matthew 7:22-23a)

Why does Satan heal? He attempts to duplicate the works of God to deceive the nations. He comes as "an angel of light," when in truth, he is the "prince of darkness."

I am saddened to say I practiced Reiki on many people, including my daughter. She had stomach aches as a small child, and I tried to relieve her discomfort by doing Reiki on her.

By doing so, it may have led to more health issues for her, including Type I Diabetes at age five. I don't know if my practice of calling on demonic powers to heal her gave her diabetes or not, but I can't help but wonder.

I believe I willingly and ignorantly opened many doors to the demonic. It's sad to know what I took part in, and what it brought upon my family. So, my purpose in writing this book is to warn others. I pray that the Lord Jesus will open your eyes to the truth and expose and dispel all darkness. I encourage you to repent of any New Age practices and experience God's healing and deliverance.

SHAMANS

Shamanism is a form of spirituality that involves the manipulation of reality to obtain benefits for the individual.

The term shaman comes from the Evenki language of Siberia and means "one who sees the source." Shamanic practices often include a variety of healing techniques and rituals. The shaman is also known by many other local names, such as sorcerer, healer, witch doctor or a walker between the worlds.

The main role of a shaman is to connect with the spirit world by conjuring up demons and working with energies in the physical world. Most shamans use drums, rattles, dance or other percussion instruments to create repetitive sounds. Through these experiences, shamans supposedly gain knowledge of the nature of sacred power.

In addition, shamans also consult with spirits to diagnose and resolve problems. They can supposedly sense feelings and retrieve messages from the dead.

Anyone who knows the truth about Jesus Christ would never call on shamans. But again, if you have, repent. He will forgive you.

SWEAT LODGES

A Sweat Lodge is an ancient Native American tradition. It comprises a circle of participants sitting around a fire pit. The structure consists of 16 willow branches with the ends buried in the ground; covered with animal hides. The participants place hot rocks inside the fire pit and recite prayers. Water is poured on the hot stones and the steam rises. The Sweat Lodge Ceremony is supposed to purify one's body of toxins, restore mental clarity, and spiritually reconnect them to the Great Spirit.

The process of the Sweat Lodge is described as a healing ritual. People enter the sweat lodge to ask for help from the Great Spirit. Prayers and songs are offered to call in helping spirits. The rhythmic beat of a drum made from natural materials is a central item in the ceremony. During the ritual, each person is allowed to speak.

Many participants describe what is to them a profound experience of both physical and spiritual cleansing. They feel like a new person once they emerge. They testify that it feels as if they are emerging from the womb. The Sweat Lodge is sometimes referred to as "the womb of Mother Earth."

Some engage in New Age practices to achieve a well-balanced life. One of the most popular is meditation.

Chapter 10

New Age Health Applications

MEDITATION

It isn't easy to define meditation because it appears in many forms and for many purposes. The definition of the term *meditation* varies from culture to culture.

New Age meditation is generally a mental exercise or discipline where one focuses on a single thing, such as breathing or the repetition of a mantra, which is a word or

sound one repeats to aid concentration, which is most often the name of a god or goddess. This mental exercise is a method to attain heightened spiritual awareness. That is because the mantras summon spirits from which they supposedly receive wisdom.

Transcendental Meditation (TM) is another practice in which I was involved. I proactively brought TM to my local community and into several people's lives. The name of the ruling spirit, given to me by my guru when he blew his breath on me while teaching me TM, was *Shring*. I was told it was my personal mantra.

I had to be delivered of this. This was a huge stronghold in my life. God revealed to me that *Shring* was the gatekeeper, keeping me in torment by allowing other demonic forces into my life. I had to repent and receive deliverance from this. I beg you, please take this seriously. To properly meditate requires one to quiet one's mind and concentrate.

WHERE DID MEDITATING ORIGINATE?

It is an ancient activity or behavior practiced by many traditions and religions, each with its own peculiarities. The New Age Movement has, as I have said, adopted certain techniques and practices from them with little consideration of the source or possible results.

WHY IS MEDITATION IMPORTANT?

The value of meditation is often underestimated. Proper meditation is said to help people calm their minds, reduce stress, achieve greater focus, be more relaxed, and have more energy. Some say it also helps them in their daily tasks and decision-making skills and improves their overall quality of life.

It sounds like a "cure-all," doesn't it? New Age meditation is believed by some to activate physical healing, cure, or reduce the risk of heart disease. Some even maintain it will cure a common cold. But most folks say it simply helps people live happier lives.

Some New Age believers say that they feel more connected to their inner selves, experience a higher level of peace, and can connect with other people on a deeper level. Properly done, it can be beneficial, but improperly done, such as focusing on an occult mantra, it can also open the door to the spirit realm that you wouldn't want to be opened.

WHAT DOES GOD SAY ABOUT IT?

While some Christians associate meditation with other world religions, we should not overlook the place of true biblical meditation.

Meditation is mentioned multiple times in the Bible. Genesis 24:63a, for instance, states, *"And Isaac went out to meditate in the fields at the eventide...."*

The Psalmist wrote, *"Let the words of my mouth, and the meditation of my heart, be acceptable in thy sight, O LORD, my strength and my redeemer."* (Psalm 19:14) And, in Joshua 1:8a, we read, *"This book of the law shall not depart out of thy mouth; but thou shalt meditate therein day and night...."*

Throughout the Psalms, there are references to meditation. But notice in the Joshua passage (above) the command was to meditate on the Word of God, day, and night. And in the New Testament, we are also instructed to *"pray without ceasing."* (1 Thessalonians 5:17). Please understand that prayer is more than talking to God; it is often (and sometimes only) listening to Him.

Though the word "meditation" does not appear in the New Testament, the Apostle Paul encourages us to focus our thinking on good things, which is essentially the same. (Philippians 4:8)

The bottom line? Meditation *is absolutely* to be part of a spiritually healthy Christian's life. It is *the focus* of one's meditation that matters most. The goal of biblical meditation is to renew our minds and make us more like Jesus. (Romans 12:1-2)

To make the most of your practice, go to a quiet place, such as a park or an isolated field. For example, you could use your car to sit in a parking lot or a conference room, where you could be alone.

Some Christians have appointed prayer places in their homes. The Bible talks about one having a prayer closet. Jesus said, *"But when you pray, go into your room, close the door, and pray to your Father, who is unseen. Then your Father, who sees what is done in secret, will reward you. Then your Father, who sees what is done in secret, will reward you."* (Matthew 6:6, NIV)

There are many ways to meditate, according to the Bible. The most popular form is reading Scripture. You can choose any version of Scripture and write down your thoughts on the verse. Some people practice the art of *Lectio Divina* (or divine reading), a type of meditative prayer. They find it beneficial.

The four steps to this kind of meditation are:
1. Read a meaningful passage (perhaps a verse or two).
2. Meditate on what you have read. Consider each word separately.
3. Pray about what you have read.
4. Then invite the Holy Spirit to speak to you, to illuminate, and apply what you have read.

Keep your pen and paper handy to write down the illumination or revelation God brings. Whereas non-Christian forms of meditation often encourage you to empty your mind of all thoughts and images, biblical meditation fills the mind with the good things. (Philippians 4:8)

WHAT DANGERS MIGHT BE INVOLVED?

The danger involved in worldly meditation relates to how it is practiced. New Age practices of meditation, like Hindu, Jainism or Buddhism techniques, use mantras, believing them to provide *spiritual power*, which is spiritually dangerous. The reason certain mantras have been passed down from generation to generation in these false religions is that the prescribed mantras summon demonic spirits.

Remember, our premise. There are only two sources of spiritual power. They are God's power, via His Holy Spirit, and satanic power via demonic spirits. So, the only way to access God's spiritual power is to meditate His way, His Word, and to engage with His Holy Spirit.

Christian meditation doesn't require a demonic mantra or an empty mind. It is meditating on God Himself, one of His promises, or one of His attributes... like His love.

Another popular New Age activity that purports to help one achieve a well-balanced life is the practice of Yoga.

YOGA

Yoga is reportedly a $4 billion industry. Nearly 10% of North Americans practice yoga. Our enemy is weaving yoga and martial arts into our society's fabric! As it is with martial arts,

there is widespread ignorance as to what it is all about.

Both yoga and martial arts have their roots in India and China. We can see that they were practiced simultaneously by people who did both. According to the Shao Lin monks' stories, they recognized the need to improve their fighting abilities and to increase their spiritual awareness through their breathing exercises.

Yoga is directly related to Hinduism, which is prevalent in India. The Western version of Hinduism in the West is disguised under New Age teachings. Yoga is just one of the tools that New Agers and others use to spread their perverted gospel throughout our country, as well as around the globe.

There are many beliefs mixed into Yoga's roots, such as yin, yang and karma. They also believe in nirvana and transcendental meditation. All of which are based on false religions. Some of these goals include:
- Self-perfection
- Wisdom
- Oneness with the universe
- Enlightenment
- Unity of mind and body through harmony between them

These are said to be achieved through the following:
- Breathing exercises
- Mantras
- Trance states of "mindlessness."
- By obtaining specific positions

These things have spiritual significance because they tap into the forbidden occult realm ruled by other gods (demonic beings). Yoga also uses specific mantras to summon Hindu gods.

The word *yoga* means "to yoke" or "to bind together." Hinduism has many practices that can be used to help one reach nirvana (a state of perfect bliss) faster and escape the endless cycle of life, or as in the case of reincarnation, lives. Meditation and Yoga are two of the most important New Age tools.

It aims to clear the mind and stop all movement in the body. Brahman, a Hindu god, is known to be "everything." Yoga's ultimate goal is to unite the practitioner with Brahman.

Interestingly, yoga means "to yoke" or "to bind together," and Scripture warns us, *"Do not be yoked together with unbelievers. For what do righteousness and wickedness have in common? Or what fellowship can light have with darkness?"* (2 Corinthians 6:14)

The truth is that the person who meditates opens their mind to demons. Students of yoga are instructed to reach out for Shiva, or "the light." In John 8:12, ESV, we read, *"Again Jesus spoke to them, saying, '****I am the light of the world****. Whoever follows me will not walk in darkness but will have the light of life."* (Emphasis added)

Yes, I am fully aware that there are churches with "Christian yoga groups." To justify it, they usually claim to practice the basic physical positions, called "Asanas," and the yoga breathing techniques called "Pranayama," which is to help "prana," the vital energy flow throughout the body. However, Scripture continually commands us to be filled with the Holy Spirit, not "prana." (Ephesians 5:18)

If you do some simple research, you will notice that the Asanas, the physical positions assumed by Yoga practitioners, including Christians, match the physical positions in depictions of Hindu gods and goddesses.

The "cobra posture" is a common yoga position. It involves lying on your stomach with your head raised. According to yoga textbooks, this position is known as the "cobra position" (cobra, as in snake), and it is a common asana.

It is believed that the person has now "liberated his spirit from the prisoner of his earthly consciousness" and entered a state of blissful oneness. Raja Yoga, the most advanced form of yoga, aims to "purify emotions and broaden the intellect" to make one think of himself as a "divine immortal being."

That certainly sounds familiar. It is almost word-for-word what Satan said in Isaiah 14:14; he longs to be God.

KUNDALINI

Kundalini is associated with yoga and life force. In Hinduism, Kundalini is a form of divine feminine energy believed to be located at the base of the spine in the Muladhara. There is a spirit attached to this word and what is taught. People want to access this for healing, but in reality, it brings death.

This spirit acts like a boa constrictor, choking the life out of a person. I have also seen a few people where their spine in the natural was affected, causing pain and paralysis versus the healing they were looking for. This is something one may need deliverance from because it likes to attach itself and work on bringing ill health, so you look even further and deeper into other gods, all the while promoting health.

I was delivered from Hatha Yoga. It is a ruling demonic entity that gained access to my life from one of the many doors I had opened in the New Age. "Hatha" was a gatekeeper to other spirits that had gained access and where Jesus had to set me free. Jesus wants you free too. You may not realize the bondage you are in, or that you have allowed this into your life. But, if you are dabbling in these practices, even if you are Christian, you need to be aware.

I know this is a touchy subject with many people, especially Christians. But this is my testimony, my story, and I would be remiss in leaving it out.

Are you seeing "the Light?" Yoga, as do other New Age practices, directs people away from our Creator and His Son, Jesus, rather than to them.

The Bible does not instruct us to clear our minds. Instead, it instructs us to *"put on the mind of Christ."* (1 Corinthians 2:16) Yoga teaches that one should empty their mind before doing yoga. This is because the one who does that lowers their will and the protection God gave them against evil influence is gone.

Another New Age tactic, which is said to help one achieve a well-balanced life, is the practice of Tai Chi.

TAI CHI

Some say, "Tai Chi is so powerful that it can heal you!" They call it "medicine in motion." It is a Chinese martial art, a system of gentle physical exercises and stretches consisting of sequences of very slow, controlled, deliberate movements. Its postures flow fluidly from one to the next without pause, which ensures that one's body is in constant motion. Tai Chi practice is thought to strengthen one's inner chi. Chi is sometimes referred to as the "supreme ultimate life force" that holds the universe together. Here again, we see a substitute for Almighty God.

As Christians, we believe God is the ultimate life force who holds all things together. The Apostle Paul wrote, *"For by him (God) all things were created, in heaven and on earth, visible and invisible, whether thrones or dominions or rulers or authorities—all things were created through him and for him. And he is before all things, and in him, all things hold together."* (Colossians 1:16–17)

Properly taught, Tai Chi is meditative, with a focus on thought and breath, and movement. However, because its origin and beliefs are based on Eastern mysticism, it is contrary to the teachings of Scripture. The ancient Chinese religion Taoism teaches there is no personal God, only a source or principle of creation. It teaches that yin and yang are forces that work together to balance the chi.

People are told they can advance this balance through diet, herbs, exercises including Tai Chi, breathing techniques, and its specific movement. Chinese philosophers consider Tai Chi the ultimate source and limit of reality, from which spring yin and yang and all of creation. Tai Chi is sometimes described as meditation in motion because it promotes serenity through gentle movements — connecting the mind and body.

Like yoga, Tai Chi also helps improve muscle tone and strength, respiration and cardio health, according to the American Osteopathic Association. It is also noted that Tai Chi improves coordination and is thought to relieve pain, although research into the effectiveness of Tai Chi for pain relief is scarce. Once yoga and Tai Chi are analyzed individually, they are virtually identical in both their benefits and components.

But is it worth it? Let's take a closer look. This gentle form of exercise has many benefits, including the ability to increase one's flexibility and strength.

Unlike other forms of exercise, Tai Chi can be practiced anytime and anywhere. However, purists maintain that it is meant to be practiced outdoors. It is difficult to learn from watching videos.

In the Far East, Tai Chi training is often practiced by older people. Some people continue practicing extreme Tai Chi forms well into their nineties. It is said to overcome depression, insomnia and other physical issues.

TAI CHI AND SCRIPTURE

Tai Chi originated in Eastern mysticism. Its full name is Tai Chi Chuan, which translates as "supreme ultimate force." Remember, there are only two sources of spiritual power in the universe, God's power and Satan's. God is the *Supreme Ultimate Force*, not Tai Chi. And as mentioned above, contrary to the Taoist teaching of Tai Chi, God Himself holds all things together.

A Christian should avoid Tai Chi. Its spiritual underpinnings are nonbiblical and anti-Christian.

Chapter 11

New Age vs. Divine Revelation

New Age beliefs, as you can see, are quite close to the truth. However, upon examination, we discover they are only "half-truths." A half-truth is a whole lie! Interestingly, since the practices originated in many cases thousands of years ago, in multiple places on earth, one should realize they are the work of a "master planner," Satan, the "father of lies." (John 8:44)

The New Age Movement—a hodgepodge of scientific hokum, heresy and deception—could emerge as the greatest threat to Christianity in history. While it claims to be new, it is as old as the Garden of Eden, with its promises that you will not die and you will be gods. New Age teaching says that we will not die; we will be reincarnated.

The Bible says that it is appointed for a man once to die, and after that comes the judgment. The New Agers teach that we are all gods. The Bible teaches that there is one God! The New Age Movement urges the abandoning of objective moral standards such as the Word of God. If we are gods, they reason, we can set our own standards of conduct." (Anonymous)

Chapter 12

10 Reasons Why the New Age Movement is Not Christian

The New Age Movement refers to a set of spiritual beliefs, practices and groups that developed in western societies during the 1970s. It refers to a range of eclectic and syncretic religious traditions, encompassing an array of beliefs from occultism to multiple forms of Eastern and Western mysticism, as well as ideas from pre-modern religions such as Neoplatonism. These beliefs influence many contemporary pagan spiritualities.

- **The New Age Movement promotes a different Jesus.**

The Christian faith, according to Scripture, proclaims that Jesus Christ was born of a virgin, lived a sinless life, and died on the cross to atone for man's sin.

It is true that many in today's culture scoff at such a claim and may even call it absurd. However, millions of Christians know full well what their faith entails, and those who are devout believers should never be apologetic about their beliefs.

- **The New Age Movement is pantheistic.**

The distinction between pantheism and Christianity is difficult, but I will attempt to be as clear as possible.

Pantheism teaches that all of reality (and everything in it) *is* God. The Christian conception of God and his relationship with us has been clearly stated in Scripture, however: *"For from him and through him and to him are all things. To him be glory forever!"* (Romans 11:36)

- **The New Age Movement focuses on self-development instead of serving others.**

"And he (Jesus) *said unto them all, 'If any man will come after me, let him deny himself, and take up his cross daily, and follow me."* (Luke 9:23). The Bible teaches that we should live for Christ rather than our own gain, and we should love one another not only with words but by serving each other in God's name.

- **The New Age Movement denies the truth about Christ.**

The New Age Movement teaches that Jesus wasn't divine, that He never claimed to be God, and that He was merely a teacher. The movement also says Jesus didn't die on the cross for man's sins; rather, he died because of Roman persecution.

- **Some core beliefs of the New Age are at odds with Christianity.**

The New Age movement believes that all religions and paths lead to God. This, however, directly contradicts Jesus, who in John 14:6 said, *"I am the way and the truth and life. And no one comes to the Father exccpt through me."*

- **The New Age Movement elevates man's opinions over God's Word.**

If one's opinion about God differs from what He has revealed in His Word, then he does not believe what God has written, which is idolatry (Romans 1:22-23). The New Age Movement exalts human opinion above that of God's revelation; therefore, it is fundamentally unchristian and contrary to Scripture.

- **The New Age Movement creates an anything-goes mentality.**

The Bible warns us about putting God to the test, but that's exactly what people do when they seek guidance through Tarot cards or their horoscopes. No matter how trendy these practices may seem, they're not God-ordained. Seeking counsel from mediums and psychics is a direct violation of Scripture and will take you down a slippery slope and away from Christ's teachings—not toward them.

- **The New Age Movement denies the necessity of Jesus' sacrificial death in payment for man's sin.**

The Bible declares that *we are all under sin* (Romans 3:23) and that *the wages of sin is death* (Romans 6:23). The only way out of that spiritual death sentence is through repentance, by which we accept what Jesus did on our behalf and place our faith in Him. According to Acts 4:12, *"There is no other name under heaven by which man must be saved."*

- **The New Age Movement is occult.**

The basic idea of many occult beliefs and practices is that people can manipulate nature, human destiny and events following their own desires or even their own whims, which is contrary to Scripture. At their root, occult beliefs are witchcraft, and witchcraft is an abomination to God. I was in complete shock when this truth was revealed to me. I would never openly agree to witchcraft, yet, there I was, totally involved and partnering with the demonic rather than with God.

- **The New Age Movement teaches God is in everything and everyone.**

The basic tenet of many false religions, including Buddhism, Hinduism and Theosophy, is that all things are God (or are part of God). Even if you say you do not believe in God and believe that He exists outside of all things (panentheism), it is still a form of monism because everything in existence shares a common essence or divine spark with every other thing.

Romans 1:28 prophesied the day would come when "*they exchanged the truth about God for a lie and worshiped and served created things rather than the Creator—who is forever praised. Amen.*"

MY RESCUE!

How did I get so deeply involved in the occult, New Age practice? Looking back, I did grow up in a church surrounded by very sincere pastors and believers. So how did I go astray and get caught up in all of this?

I sensed the Holy Spirit early on as a child, and I am so grateful I did. However, later I sensed other spirits as well. I didn't know what to do with those experiences. It was not taught or talked about in the church I grew up in. Once or twice, I attended a Pentecostal church, but I was quite fearful. I have often wished someone had talked to me about the Holy Spirit and how to react to the evil, unseen spirit world.

Because I didn't learn that Christ had died for me to free me from condemnation, I was being taught by the unseen realm. My ability to discern spiritual entities was a gift. It was a gift from God. But the enemy knew it too and went after me hard. I could see and hear from the spirit realm, but it was the wrong realm.

But Jesus!

So, when the Bates's started picking me up for church, I heard the messages, and though a child, I took them seriously. God was speaking to me. I didn't read the Bible a lot, but when

I did, it was the Book of Esther, one of only two books in the Bible named for women. I loved the story of Esther.

It was the book that was the least condemning to me as I read it. It also really built me up and gave me hope. It pointed to a savior. And helped instill in me a hope and a future. It was also a story that didn't frighten me or cause me to think I was going to hell. That is the truth.

I heard a lot of things in church that I interpreted to mean that because I could never be good enough to go to heaven, I would surely go to hell. Let me tell you, my friend—if this is you, there is good news. You don't have to be good enough. You cannot be good enough... no one can. You must simply receive God's free gift—eternal life in Christ Jesus. (See below)

I continued to have a lot of condemnation, though, growing up and into my twenties and thirties. I liked the New Age teachings because they were more about self-help, healing, and evolving. That was what I wanted to hear. It was encouraging to me and gave me hope. I was not hearing hope in the church.

I am not bashing the church. It was my tainted view of the church and the Word and Jesus that was wrong. I came to know I need like-minded people and fellowship with others who are following Christ. But during my 20 years as a New Age practitioner, I did not know this.

When I was about 18, I went off to college, and this is where I was first exposed to New Age beliefs and teachings. The internet was just taking off, and searching for things became a lot easier to do. When I would google "hearing things," "seeing things," or "knowing things," the search would always return New Age information. It didn't mention anything about spiritual gifts from the Bible. It gave me options to look at which were outside of God's Word. So, of course, that is the direction I moved in.

As I said previously, the deeper I got into New Age practices, the more it drew me in. I was involved in almost all the things mentioned in the previous chapters to one degree or another, and others not listed.

So, how did I escape New Age teaching and practices? It started with my visit to a Christian OB/GYN (a doctor who specializes in women's health), who addressed the depression I had dealt with for 20 years. She said that Jesus was a healer (or something to that effect). I proudly told her I was not a religious person, but I was spiritual, and I briefly described my path. She graciously said to me that Jesus wasn't religious either and that it was the religious people who killed Him.

She went on to tell me the Bible was one of the most spiritual books ever written. I looked at her like they had slapped me. It was a gut punch. I left that appointment and went home to check out the Bible and try to read it again. It was about the same time that the events I mention at the beginning of this book were happening. I was looking for answers. Real answers. Ones that worked. Ones that were powerful.

I found that power. The power I had been looking for the last 20 years. In His mercy, Jesus showed up and rescued me. He walked me through deliverance, through His Word, and through the most difficult time in my life. He stood beside me, taught me, and equipped me to come out of the battle I was in. He did for me what I could not do for myself. Plus, He equipped me to run back into the fire and help rescue those who are being consumed by the flames. May you find Him today!

  I was rescued and you can be, too!

Chapter 13

Not All Roads Lead to Heaven—This One Does!

Do you know Jesus? If not, you can meet Him today. Each of us has sinned. To sin is to "miss the mark." Sin is an old archery term. The red and white concentric rings around the bullseye, on the target, are called "sins."

By repenting of your sin and trusting Jesus Christ to be your Lord and Savior, you can come to know Him personally. Jesus Christ died on the cross for your sins and mine. He was buried and rose again three days later for our justification. Forty days later, He ascended into heaven, where He presented His blood on our behalf.

Jesus is the unique mediator between God and man. Come to Christ today. Let Him forgive you, cleanse you, and renew your heart. This good news is your do-over!

Have you watched a television show called "Extreme Makeover?" That makeover, of course, has to do with changing a person's physical imperfections to make them more attractive.

When a friend of mine was in college, one of the campus beauties wrote in his yearbook, "May only the beauty of Jesus be seen in us." Perhaps your life is a real mess today. I want you to know that Jesus Christ can do an extreme makeover in your life.

In 2 Corinthians 5:17, we read, *"If any man* (person) *be in Christ, he is a new creation."* Come to Jesus today. Allow Him to forgive, cleanse, and transform you—to make you over again!

EPILOGUE

If you sense God speaking to your heart right now, He is calling you into His Kingdom. Take a moment and speak to Him from your heart with this simple prayer:

"Lord, I need you.
I have sinned against you.
I understand that the price of sin is death.
Jesus, I believe you died in my place.
I believe you rose again three days later.
Living Christ, I ask you to come into my heart.
Set up your Kingdom in me.
You are my Lord, Jesus. YOU are my Lord.
Thank you for saving me.
Amen."

Read Romans 3:23, 6:23, 5:8, 10:9-10,13, and Revelation 3:20 for clarity on the steps you have just taken.

www.ingramcontent.com/pod-product-compliance
Lightning Source LLC
Chambersburg PA
CBHW051551010526
44118CB00022B/2657